CW00403034

The Crowther Centre Monograph. ... _ .... aiming to promote missiological research at a serious yet accessible level. These will be occasional publications addressing current issues in mission. They aim not only to inform but also to transform as writers present a summary of the implications of their research.

We hope that as various issues in mission are explored in this series, they will challenge and enhance not only our understanding of God, but also our engagement with God's world. Missiology, or the study of issues in mission, is an applied and engaged discipline. It is a discipline that encourages us to be active and involved so that we live out a theology of the road rather than one of the balcony. Missiology also draws on other disciplines – it is wide ranging and eclectic as it seeks to understand the implications of working out God's mission in an increasingly complex and globalised world. And finally, missiology is an incomplete discipline – as it seeks to reflect on the practice of mission, it will always be developing. So there is no such thing as a definitive missiology – there is only missiology in progress.

May you enjoy and be challenged as you read these essays and may they open up new vistas and expanding horizons for you as you journey in God's mission in the world today.

DR CATHY ROSS
MANAGER FOR CROWTHER CENTRE FOR MISSION EDUCATION

A Biblical Basis for Project Evaluation

Dr. Johan P. Velema[1]
The Leprosy Mission International
December 2008

Introduction

As so many Christian organisations, like The Leprosy Mission (TLM), are confronted with the need to formalise their activities and adhere to – and be seen to be adhering to – professional standards, the need for evaluation of our work is growing. This is also true where funds are sought from large institutional donors including governments, these funds are released on condition that formal evaluation will take place. For TLM, this is true in the area of health and development in countries where leprosy is endemic, but also in the area of making its work known through the media and raising funds. Getting involved in evaluation as Christian organisations, what is more natural than to ask how we can do this in conformity to our Christian values? Coming from a reformed background, I strongly believe that Jesus is Lord over every area of our individual and collective lives. The word of God is about real people in the real world and will be relevant to our reality – our work as much as our spirituality – if we have eyes to see it. And so it makes sense to ask what the bible says about evaluation.

The ideas expressed in this paper have been formed over a seven year period during which I was head of the Evaluation and Monitoring Service of The Leprosy Mission International. During the training courses, which were designed to help Mission staff – doctors, therapists, social workers – to become effective project evaluators, we would read the bible together and discuss how the bible speaks into our reality of work and service, responsibility, authority, of being an expert, and of affirming or criticising the work of others.

We will go step by step, first outlining the cycle of project planning, considering some essential ingredients of evaluation and then thinking about the biblical material relevant to these areas and to the person engaged in these activities.

1 I am grateful to both TLM and CMS for giving me the opportunity to intermittently spend time at the Crowther Centre for Mission Education in 2008. Besides a time of enrichment through personal study, this was also an opportunity to initiate a process of publication of which this paper is the result. Correspondence: irdo@tlmi.nl or PO Box 902, 7301 BD Apeldoorn, Netherlands.

Project planning

Simply stated, a development project is an investment aimed at transforming an unhappy situation into a happier one. In an area where there is leprosy, a project can be aimed at helping health workers recognise its symptoms, administer treatment and refer the patient if complications occur. Another project may bring together persons with disabilities, including those affected by leprosy, in self-help groups in which they exchange experiences and develop ideas to improve their own situation, including the generation of income. Where such activities are small in terms of the number of people and the resources involved, not much planning may be needed. As projects grow in size, however, and financial resources are sought from external donors, formal planning and project documentation become mandatory.

Of course, a project can only address one or a few issues at a time and has to be focussed on a defined target group. Therefore, the first step in developing a project plan is to study and analyse a situation to decide what is really needed here. The next step is to make choices, ideally with the participation of all concerned, about what problems or which target group will be addressed first. Detailed plans are developed and written up and the resulting project proposal will be submitted to committees and agencies who are in a position to release money for the execution of these plans. This, of course, is an important phase where many will comment on the feasibility of the proposed plans and suggest adaptations to increase the chances of success.

When all these phases have been worked through, the planned project will be implemented and this requires the usual management activities of recruiting and supervising staff, organising logistical support, managing financial resources, making work plans, monitoring progress and reporting to stakeholders[2] .

It is only after a prolonged period of implementation and monitoring that evaluation appears on the horizon. Evaluation helps the people involved in the project to see whether the intended aims of the project have been realised and what may have helped or hindered the realisation of the project aims. The evaluation findings will provide a basis for deciding what to do next. As further plans are formulated to improve performance or to address different problems or to take the successes achieved to

---

2 All those who have a direct interest in the success or failure of a project – those who have a stake in it – are the stakeholders. They usually include the donor agency, the executing agency, the project staff, the target group, the local or national government.

different areas, the cycle of project planning is repeated (cf. Figure 1)

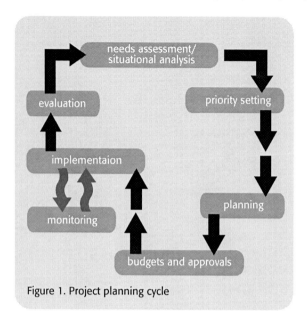

Figure 1. Project planning cycle

Project Evaluation

There are many opinions on what evaluation should be and how it should be done. In fact, there is no 'one size fits all' in evaluation and I have always prepared evaluations individually, defining purpose, expected outcomes, people to be included in the process, methods and logistics specifically for the project to be evaluated and for the situation in which it finds itself at that particular time. Even so, there are essential ingredients in evaluation that will always be there, no matter how much variation is introduced. In a brochure published by the Swedish Mission Council , evaluation is defined as "a systematic inquiry into the worth and merit of an object". This minimalist definition says that evaluation involves systematic enquiry - collecting quantitative and qualitative data, interviewing key persons representing different interest groups, whether or not with a direct link to the project, going through historical data or reports etc. so that whatever is concluded is based on observations, on data and on evidence of what happened.

EVALU-ation is also assigning a value to the work that has been done and to the changes it has brought about. Of course, it is increasingly recognised that different stakeholders may well attach a different value to the project evaluated. The funders, the managers, the members of the target group and numerous other parties may have strong opinions about what was good or what was bad in the experience they all had. This will depend on differences in perceptions but also on different needs and interests. One stakeholder may dominate the evaluation process and elevate his value above the values assigned by others. The evaluation could result in a negotiation between stakeholders about the different values they attach to the project and decide together how the next step should take multiple views into account (SMC, 2003).

Evaluation is part of a decision making process concerning the actions to be taken in the life of the project. That process has political aspects and will not only be based on technical information. Evaluation should make the best possible contribution to this process by providing sound information, presenting different points of view and by being transparent about the reasoning by which conclusions were reached and recommendations formulated.

Evaluation Process

Evaluation is a process that happens in phases over a period of 3 to 6 months[3] . It involves a preparation phase where the purpose is defined, evaluators are contracted, information is gathered and methods are decided. Good communication between all parties concerned is vital so that no misunderstandings arise about what will happen and why. The timing of project visits is also very important both in terms of where the project is in its planning cycle and so as to minimise the burden to the project staff and target group. A written Terms of Reference embodies the choices made and the agreements reached between stakeholders.

Evaluators will be selected on the basis of their evaluation skills and the technical expertise needed as defined by the purpose of the evaluation. Ideally a balanced team

---

3 This process has been current in The Leprosy Mission between 2000 and 2007. At the time of writing, alternative approaches to evaluation are being explored which will result in processes of which the details are different from what is described here. The kind of work being done, the themes addressed, the financial investments made, the stakeholders involved will all have an influence on the final form of the evaluation process, including its duration. This does not in any way invalidate the biblical principles presented, although their application may differ in different contexts.

should incorporate different points of view and therefore include different disciplines, genders, nationalities, abilities etc. Of course, the size of the team can only be limited and choices have to be made. One such choice concerns the question whether evaluators should be internal or external to the implementing organisation. Institutional donors will often require that evaluators are external and independent while others would argue that this will only increase fear and the potential for misunderstanding.

Well-prepared evaluators already know a lot about the project they are visiting and are able to ask pertinent questions, have meaningful discussions and facilitate processes that focus on the issues that count. For them, the project visit allows them to interpret the information they have received about the project and to fill gaps in their knowledge. Through such a personal visit, the project becomes the life and work of real people and not just facts on a piece of paper.

By whatever route, the evaluation will eventually lead to conclusions about the value of the work that has been done and the evaluators will formulate recommendations, taking into account all that they have seen and heard. The reporting phase is to document the evaluation process including relevant observations, interpretations, conclusions and recommendations. After that it is up to the stakeholders to take action, whether in line with the recommendations or otherwise.

Phases in an evaluation process
- ■ **Preparation:** terms, team, time
- ■ **Project visit:** observation, interpretation
- ■ **Evaluation:** conclusion, recommendation
- ■ **Reporting**
- ■ **Decision making/action**

Biblical Basis
Project Planning Cycle

Considering the various steps in the project planning cycle, we can find biblical examples of people doing similar things. *Nehemiah* studied the state of the walls of Jerusalem (2:13-15, situational analysis) and mobilised the human and material resources to rebuild them (Neh 3). *Joseph* presented a rough outline of a disaster-preparedness plan to Pharaoh (Gen 41:33-36) which was approved (37) and funded and of which he was put in charge (40-42). Joseph then went on to implement the project (46-48), monitoring it until his accounting staff was overwhelmed by its success (49). The long-term impact of the project was that many lives, both human and animal, were saved (47:25). We find that *Jesus* applied strategic thinking to his mission to reach the nation, setting up his base in Capernaum (Lk 4:31), then leaving this base again (Lk 4:42-44), travelling around Judea (4:44, 8:1) and multiplying his efforts by training his disciples to do the same (9:1-6) and then training an even greater number and sending them out as well (Lk 10). The apostle *Paul* developed a strategy to reach the provincial capitals of the Roman Empire, counting on the self-propagating churches he founded to reach the rest of the province (Allen, 1927)

Thus activities such as needs assessment, planning, strategy development and implementation are not outside the reality encountered in biblical times. Historically, leaders in the old and new testaments used these skills to do God's work and to serve **the people he created.** Being guided by the Holy Spirit and working within a stated strategy are not opposites. Rather, over-emphasising one at the expense of the other is counter-productive.

Evaluation

After such a lead-in it will come as no surprise that I have found numerous examples in the bible of people who evaluated their work. When Luther said that we should be carpenters, blacksmiths and mathematicians after God (McGrath, 2007), he could have perfectly well added: and evaluators after God. Right in the first chapter of the bible, at the beginning of the world, we read that the Almighty considered the work of his hands and seven times evaluated His creation as good and even very good (Gn 1: 4, 10, 12, 18, 21, 25, 31). In the following, we will see that we find our lived reality of project evaluation reflected back to us in the bible and that there are lessons we can learn through this.

In a general sense, all our work is taking place in human history, which is unfolding between the starting point of the Fall and the endpoint of the apocalypse i.e. the transformation of the world from its present shape into a new creation. Our present reality and our work are affected by sin and a disturbed relationship between God and ourselves. Our knowledge is partial (1 Cor 13:9), our actions are hindered by bodies that are subject to sickness and death (1 Cor 15:43) and by a will that is unable to adhere to good principles (Rom 7:21-22). And so it is realistic to evaluate our work and expect to find shortcomings and even total failures. Imperfect knowledge, imperfect communication and imperfect action all contribute to this and we should sometimes remind ourselves that perfection is only found in God. This is not to say we should not strive for quality in our work with all our might, all the more so because we believe our work will be transformed and become incorporated into the new creation (1 Cor 3:10-15, Rietkerk, 1989).

The twelve explorers (Numbers 13)

A surprising amount of detail has been preserved of the first reconnaissance party that the people of Israel sent out into the land of Canaan[4]. There is a detailed description of the team members (verses 1-16), all heads of families (or clans), carefully chosen to represent each of the tribes. I am grateful to my colleagues for pointing out to me that this, of course, was a way of ensuring that the recommendations resulting from the exercise would be more easily accepted by all tribes.

There is a detailed instruction concerning the data the team needed to collect (17-20):

"Go up through the Negev and on into the hill country. See what the land is like and whether the people who live there are strong or weak, few or many. What kind of land do they live in? Is it good or bad? What kind of towns do they live in? Are they unwalled or fortified? How is the soil? Is it fertile or poor? Are there trees on it or not? Do your best to bring back some of the fruit of the land." (NIV)

The questions were formulated specifically for this situational analysis and are relevant to the decisions and planning the Israelites would have to make to prepare for a military campaign and for settling their people in the land. Thus the purpose of the exploration was clearly defined through these questions as well.

We are then given a description (21-25) of the duration of the exploration mission, the route travelled and some of the places visited. It is clear that this was a thorough exercise undertaken with a large team and covering a large territory from the south to the very north of the land.

---

4 For some readers the entry of the people of Israel into Canaan represents an act of unlawful aggression. The present application of the story does not include a value judgment of the conquest of Canaan but only seeks to draw out practical lessons - just like the strategies of the German army in World War II can provide lessons for us today regardless of whether we consider their campaigns at the time as a good or a bad thing.

The explorers completed their trip and then came back and reported their findings, exactly under the two headings which made up the dual purpose of this exercise. Concerning the suitability of the land as a future home they all agreed that it was a fertile and desirable land (26-27). Concerning the military aspect, the evaluators agreed on what they had seen and mapped out the cities and the different populations (28-29), but when it came to interpretation of these observations, they differed among themselves and brought out a majority and a minority report. The majority recommended aborting the plans for an attack on the land (31); the minority recommended moving forward with the conquest (30). We then see that the rumours which begin to circulate about the evaluation findings are quite inaccurate compared to the report that was presented: the land devours those living in it and all the people we saw are of great size (32).

As with evaluations today, a decision making process then follows (Numbers 14). Because of the controversy, this particular process was characterised by the circulation of rumours, by strong emotions, even threats. Divine intervention is needed to protect Moses and Aaron and Moses enters into a dialogue with the Lord in order to find a way forward. It becomes clear that God rejects the majority report and supports the expression of faith embedded in the minority report. God gives the people what they want and it becomes their curse. The evaluators who presented the majority report come to their death soon after this (14:37), thus showing that the responsibility of the evaluator is a matter that should not be taken lightly. Although I do not think this means that evaluators should expect sudden death if they make a mistake, it does serve as a reminder that our work will one day be tested – evaluated by our Master (1 Cor 3:10-15) - and that faith comes into our valuation of a project and not just technical considerations *per se*.

The lessons for our current evaluation practice are many and varied. Transparency is important, and involving people from the start. There is an art to choosing team members. Giving clear instructions to evaluators is an important condition for the success of the exercise. Observations and their interpretation are two different things and this is perhaps the most central lesson from the story. Evaluators must become aware of how they themselves reason and move from observations to conclusions and that faith has a role to play in that process. There are also some important lessons here about the reactions an evaluator may expect if the conclusions are painful. "Do not be frightened!" (1 Pet 3:14) but rather apply all your skill to influence the decision making process for good. Making a clear presentation of the evaluation findings is the first step in such a process.

Revelation 2-3

During evaluation training courses, we read the letters to the seven churches, dictated by the Lord Jesus in a vision to John the evangelist, as if they were evaluation reports. All letters follow the same consistent structure:

- Statement on the nature of the author
- Strengths
- Points for improvement
- Recommendation for change
- Potential long-term outcome

Without going into the detailed content of these letters, it is good to see that they are written in a positive tone, showing appreciation and understanding as well as stern rejection of what is wrong, yet always seeking to show a way forward and a promise of eventual glory for those who persevere. Similarly, evaluators can seek to be positive, show appreciation and understanding while at the same time verbalising problems clearly and succinctly as well as pointing a way forward and giving hope for what can be achieved.

Do not judge (Matthew 7)

> "Do not judge so that you will not be judged. For in the way you judge, you will be judged; and by your standard of measure, it will be measured to you."
> (Matt 7:1-2, NASU)

We cannot live without judging. In order to survive, we have to constantly evaluate the signals that come to us through our senses and discern what is good, what constitutes a threat, whom we can trust and whom we should keep our distance from. In our daily lives, we have to evaluate the various offers made to us through advertising in the media, in shops and by sales persons and accept some and reject others. When reviewing the scientific literature, I have to evaluate research and decide, based on more or less objective criteria, what I am going to believe and what I am going to disregard. This means we make judgments, inevitably and constantly. Yet the Lord Jesus taught us not to judge. How can this be? How can I encourage my colleagues to evaluate the work of their peers while bound to such a command?

Realistically, I do not think Jesus meant for us to stop discerning and evaluating. However, he did warn us to exercise extreme caution when doing so. In the parallel passage in Luke, he precedes this command by the injunction to be merciful (6:36) and follows it by saying: "Do not condemn and you will not be condemned" (6:37). Condemnation is obviously an extreme type of judgment, which may on rare occasions be needed but is usually avoidable if we look into the matter more closely. Jesus himself, of course, operated in an environment which was highly judgmental and he had to constantly defend himself and explain his reasons for doing and saying the things he said and did. He knew the damage that unfounded judgments could cause both to himself and to others.

In theory: how to judge fairly?

His response was to remind us that we should not expect ourselves to escape the judgment we apply to others and so He encouraged us to become aware of the standards we use when we make judgments. The apostle Paul, incidentally, applied the same logic when he explained in his letter to the Romans that we are all under God's judgment (Rom 2) and that God will apply the standards to us that we applied to others. The Lord detests those who employ double standards, one set for their friends and another for their customers (Deut 25:13-16).

The concept of forgiveness is the logical complement to these ideas. Even a modest amount of self-knowledge will reveal just how much we fall short of God's standards in our lives and to what extent we need to call upon the grace of God and our neighbour to continue to be accepted. This humility will translate into a greater leniency towards the mistakes of others (Lk 11:4). Looking at ourselves will make us more gentle (Gal 6:1) and the measure we apply to others more generous (Lk 6:38). This does not mean that forgiveness is an excuse to gloss over problems and mistakes. Rather, it is a necessary condition for being able to face the guilt and shame of our mistakes and find solutions to the problems caused by them.

In practice: how to arrive at a fair conclusion?

During evaluation training courses we spent time reflecting on the standards we use to evaluate our work. Our motto was: to Evaluate is to Compare. Very often we will say that things are so much better than when we started (a comparison in time), or that this project runs so much more smoothly than a similar project in a neighbouring province (a comparison in space). We compare achievements with the project goals formulated in the project proposal, or we consider how the project process reflects the values of the donor agency, such as gender balance, care for the environment, inclusion of persons with disabilities etc. However, we also – often unconsciously – apply cultural and professional norms which have been transmitted to us during our childhood and education. When we started out working we were motivated by personal ideologies, religious or otherwise, which will greatly influence how we value the effects of our work and that of others.

Thus I encourage evaluators to be as transparent as possible and formulate the steps through which they arrive at the valuation of a project. What did I see or hear (observation)? what did that tell me and what did I compare this to (interpretation)? Why do I feel that that is good - or bad (conclusion)? Growing as an evaluator means to become more and more clearly aware of one's own standards and to become better able to communicate those to others. The exhortations in the old testament to use honest weights rather than to seek personal gain by using different sets for different people, take on a new meaning here (Lev 19:35-36, Deut 25:13-16, Prov 20:10, 23).

Hindrances to fair judgment

In reality, of course, we are often blind to the standards we apply. That is perhaps why Jesus added a little illustration to his words on being cautious in judging others:

> "And why do you look at the speck that is in your brother's eye, but do not notice the log that is in your own eye? Or how can you say to your brother, 'Let me take the speck out of your eye,' and behold, the log is in your own eye? You hypocrite, first take the log out of your own eye, and then you will see clearly to take the speck out of your brother's eye." (Matt 7:3-5, NASU)

This illustration is not really about our reasoning or about being reason-able. It speaks to our attitude. Why are we so adamant that the speck in our brother's eye be identified and made known? Is it to show off our professional capacity? Is it to make a big deal out of our courage to 'not budge an inch in the face of what others think' (Lk 20:21 TLB)? Is it to get even for something our brother (or our organisation) did to us in another context? Is it to pull rank at the expense of others? Is it to show our superior dedication? The list of possible 'logs in our own eye' is endless. We can be so right technically, yet so wrong to make our insight the absolute. For have we truly understood all the aspects of this problem? Have we really grasped why the plan could not be executed as agreed? Is the zig-zag path really less acceptable than the highway to success we would have liked to see?

I have found over the years that the most important distinction between a good and an average evaluator is in the attitude. An evaluator who enjoys identifying mistakes is a pain. An evaluator who does not lose any sleep over a negative conclusion will often not be able to persuade his colleagues to make changes and adjust their work plans. Such a big part of the evaluation work is to persuade the stakeholders of the need to make changes and this is often only possible if the attitude of the evaluator is one of humility and gentleness, coupled with real expertise on and insight in the issues involved.

To address this, we study the second letter to the Corinthians about the **strained** relationship that the apostle Paul had with the church in Corinth and his attitude in that situation.

Attitude: The apostle Paul (2 Corinthians)

Paul's Project:

First, it is important to see that Paul implemented a project with a clear aim: to plant Christian churches throughout the Roman empire. He had a clear strategy with a clear indicator of progress: the number (or proportion) of provincial capitals that had a church. When we study his approach to this work we see that it was characterised by prayer, team work, willingness to suffer, openness to adjust the action as the Spirit directed. The churches were made autonomous very quickly as elders were appointed and Paul relinquished authority over them (Allen, 1927). When he did not agree with what went on in a church, he could not issue commands but only seek to convince and persuade. Paul kept in touch with the young churches through visits, visits of his team members, through letters and through meeting with delegations from the churches that came to him. It is interesting to note that the second and third missionary journeys were initiated out of a desire to re-visit and strengthen the churches that had been started previously (Acts 15:36, 18:23). And so Paul was a man with a mission, a frequent traveller, who did his work with all his heart, intellect and strength – a work that cost him everything.

Criticisms against Paul

In this context, it was disconcerting for Paul that his relationship with the Christians in Corinth was quickly deteriorating. Commentators suggests that Paul had paid Corinth a brief visit during which he had given a negative evaluation concerning ideas and practices prevalent in the Corinthian church and recommending corrective action (Scott, 1998; Tasker, 1963). This had not been appreciated by the church members and the result was a flood of criticism being poured out over the evaluator. Afterwards he wrote to them, again stating the same things and possibly commenting on the discussions that had taken place when he was with them and where he had been heavily criticised and even insulted. Then Titus visited Corinth and Paul wrote 2 Corinthians when he had heard Titus report about his visit. The letter shows us 'in mirror image' as it were the concerns the Corinthians had.

Many Corinthians felt that Paul was trying to control them from a distance with stiff letters although he would never have used the same tone had he been with them (10:1, 10:10-11); they were upset that he had cancelled his next planned visit (1:17, 23); they questioned his motives and his authority (1:17, 3:5, 10:2, 13:3) and felt betrayed that he who had lived with them and had apparently been so close to them, now turned against them (7:8). There was concern that somehow Paul and his co-workers took material advantage of the Corinthians (2:17, 7:2, 12:17) and some negatively compared him to the more powerful preachers that had succeeded him (5:12, 11:4-6, 13:3), questioning his spirituality. And so the relationship between Paul and the Corinthians, which had once been so warm, had become confused and riddled with doubts and question marks. With Paul at a distance, juggling the problems of Corinth with plenty of other stresses and strains, how was he going to re-establish the relationship once again?

It is interesting to note that such accusations could easily be levelled against a travelling evaluator as well. It is often easy to question the motives and authority of a so-called expert who comes in for only a short time, sometimes unexpectedly cancels a planned visit, who may be kind and warm in personal contact but often writes reports that are critical and unrelenting. Often evaluators earn good money for their services, are frequent travellers who enjoy generous travel allowances – often paid for from the project budget. Although they often are professing Christians, their brand of Christianity may well differ from the style local Christians are used to and so it may be hard to tally faith with works, leading to even more misunderstanding. It is sometimes hard for project staff to feel they are taken seriously and this will compromise the acceptance of the advice given.

Paul's response

The second letter to the Corinthians is Paul's most personal letter, charged with emotion, expressing his hurt and pleading for their acceptance of him (6:11-13) as well as showing his uninhibited affection for them. Paul bears his soul to the Corinthians and appeals to their hearts, perhaps even more than counting on his arguments to convince them and win them over.

Paul begins by speaking of his sincerity in all that he has done and does in relation to the Corinthians. He claims that he has acted with 'simplicity and sincerity' towards them (1:12 KJV), that speaking the word of God to them is not a performance but something he does with sincerity (2:17), knowing that 'all the truth about us will be brought out in the law court of Christ' (5:10, JB). And so Paul appeals to their conscience, to their hearts, saying that deep down they know of his sincerity, 'who he really is' (5:11, JB) (cf. 3:1-3, 4:2).

Paul shows that he really cares for the Corinthians. He tells them about his own pain, even his tears, when previously writing to them (2:4). He tells them about his inability to carry on his work because of his anxiety over the difficulties that had arisen (2:12-13).

Paul assures the Corinthians that he is not seeking power but that he wants to work with them, alongside them, for the success of their life as a church together (1:24). He points to Christ as the one who ultimately holds power in their midst and calls himself and his team their servants (4:5) – a word that in that time and culture may well have been more significant than in western culture today. This servant-role is not only an inner attitude but is expressed in tangible experiences of powerlessness (6:3-10).

Paul goes to some length to explain that he did not live at their expense but rather accepted support from other churches (11:8) and intends to do the same thing again on his next visit (12:14-15). He emphasizes that Titus has acted along the same lines (12:18).

Perhaps the hardest thing for anyone is to counter accusations relating to one's personal faith. Paul does not shrink away from even this issue and solves it by giving a hint of the extra-ordinary spiritual experiences with which he has been blessed

(12:1-4) as well as of expressions of spiritual power in the past (12:12) but most of all emphasising his suffering (11: 23-27) and weakness (12:5-10), thus refusing to be drawn into the competition of spiritual authority that appears to be going between different teachers in Corinth (11:20-21, 13:3). Instead, Paul points to God's saving interventions in situations of extreme difficulty as the signs of true spirituality.

Finally, Paul speaks of his authority as an apostle of Christ. He holds on to this God-given vocation (3:6, 4:1, 6:1), claiming that he has lived up to it (12:11-12) but at the same time showing that the authority that can be derived from it is qualified and therefore limited. It is an authority to build up and not to pull down (10:8, 13:10). Paul is quoting the prophet Jeremiah here (Jer 1:10) and saying that the era of the gospel of grace is the era of which Jeremiah spoke (Jer 31:28) and in which God seeks to restore his people and draw them to himself and give them *shalom*. Thus his calling as an apostle in this era of grace is not to bring judgment but on the contrary to do what he can to build up and to seek what is good for the church.

And so, although Paul goes to great lengths to counter the criticisms levelled against him, he does not withdraw from the position he had taken concerning the problems he had identified in the Corinthian church. Although he expresses his willingness to forgive those who had been in the wrong (2:10), he sticks to his earlier conclusions and seeks to persuade the Corinthians rather than to change his conclusions.

The lessons to be drawn from this for the attitude of an evaluator are simply these: evaluators should cultivate a genuine love for the people they evaluate, should act with simplicity and sincerity in all they do, should not live at other's expense, should be willing to be servants of Christ and their colleagues, accepting hardship where this cannot be avoided, and should use their power for building up and not for pulling down. Sometimes this may involve accepting criticism and sticking to one's evaluation in a spirit of forgiveness and humility. It is not within the scope of this paper to elaborate in detail the practical application of these principles, but rest assured that this is often not as straightforward as one might at first think.

Paul's Impact

We catch a glimpse of the impact of Paul's apologia to the Corinthians in chapter 7. Admittedly we know little of how the relationship developed after Paul wrote 2

Corinthians to them. However, we do read that Titus came back speaking of the changes he had seen among many of the Corinthians already:

> ... *your suffering led to your repentance (led to a change in behaviour). Yours has been a kind of suffering that God approves, and so you have come to no kind of harm from us. To suffer in God's way means changing for the better and leaves no regrets, but to suffer as the world knows suffering brings death. Just look at what suffering in God's way has brought you; what keenness, what explanations, what indignation, what alarm! Yes, and what aching to see me, what concern for me and what justice done! In every way, you have shown yourselves blameless in this affair. (7:8-11, JB)*

Short-term sadness and long-term improvement - changes in behaviour, changes for the better, justice done and the relationship with the evaluator restored! Those are the results any evaluator would wish to see in a project that s/he evaluated.

Dr Johan Velema is an epidemiologist and public health specialist. He is working with The Leprosy Mission in research & development and based in the Netherlands. He has published a series of papers on community-based rehabilitation.

References

Allen R. *Missionary methods, St. Paul's or ours. A study of the church in the four provinces.* London: Robert Scott, 1927.

McGrath AE. *Christian theology: An introduction.* Oxford: Blackwell, 2007.

Scott JM. 2 Corinthians. *New International Biblical Commentary.* Mass, USA: Hendrickson, 1998.

SMC. "Directions for SMCs work with evaluations. Swedish Mission Council"; Sundyberg, 2003.

Tasker RVG. *2 Corinthians.* Tyndale New Testament Commentaries. Leicester: IVP, 1963.

Rietkerk W. *The future great planet earth.* Mussoorie, India: Good Books, 1989.

Abbreviations

CMS – Church Mission Society
JB - Jerusalem Bible
KJV - King James Version
NASU - New American Standard version - Updated
NIV - New International Version
SMC – Swedish Mission Council
TLB - The Living Bible
TLM – The Leprosy Mission